Contents

Contents

A guide to this book

John Hattie, *Visible Learning*, Routledge, 2009.

Whenever there is a major transition in schools, then the key success factor is whether a child makes a friend in the first month.

John Hattie (2009), quoting Galton (1995)

This book is for teachers who want to support their pupils when they move within or between schools. This may mean they are changing year group, starting secondary school or arriving from another country, perhaps halfway through the school year.

The book is concerned with practice, not policy. It's full of things to do instead of theories to ponder. One piece of research has sneaked in, but that's fine because it's fundamental to understanding transition and I've only given it a couple of paragraphs anyway.

I want you to use this book to make learning more effective and enjoyable – specifically at those key moments in their lives when children leave your care or when they stumble fresh faced through your classroom door. Whether their arrival or departure is planned or unexpected, use the thinking and activities that follow to give them the best shot you can as they make their way through school.

Section 1, Essentials, defines transition in all its breadth and depth. It's not only about moving from primary to secondary school. A wider understanding will help you to plan effectively for any and all transitions, whether your learners are starting school or moving to sixth form. Then I'll tell you about Galton's five bridges model (the research to which Hattie refers above) so you can use it to think about the nitty gritty of planning and leading a transition programme.

In **Section 2, Learning**, I summarise how children change and grow – especially with regard to their brains – so that we can tweak our teaching and expectations to match. I introduce the Personal Learning Profile, a document that helps pupils and teachers understand unique learning preferences and offers continuity and security through transition.

Then in **Section 3, Leading**, there's advice for those of you who have the challenge of planning and/or running a finely crafted sequence of transition events.

To support you with this, **Section 4, Lessons**, is packed with inclusive activities customised especially for transition. Each of the 15 activities is described, then applied to different types of transition: from starting school to leaving for university, with moving to secondary school in between.

Finally, in **Section 5, Next Steps**, I'll take a look at an undervalued yet extremely important transition: from Year 11 to Year 12. A final staging post, it may be between education and the world of work and/or between living at home and moving to living independently.

Section 1
Essentials

A definition of transition

Transition: **Passage from one form, state, style, or place to another.**

Transition, transfer, transformation, transmission and transmutation are related yet distinct words. They express different degrees of movement and change.

Human transitions

In our lifetimes we humans make many transitions. We are all born and we all die. Almost all of us start school, make friends, change school, move school again, go to college and start work. Many of us form serious relationships, produce more humans, change jobs, move house and get promoted or sacked. Some of us form new serious relationships, buy fast cars, move country and come back again. Most of us lose relatives and welcome new family members. Then we may begin to wear out, slow down, and move to hospital or care home before we die, the ultimate transition. Throughout, our bodies and minds evolve, and our beliefs and values are transformed as we find out what life is about and learn how to make the most of what's been given to us.

When we recognise the features of our own transitions we can empathise with pupils' specific educational ones.

Educational transitions

Transition in an educational context means progression to the next year group. *Transfer* is a special case of transition that involves a change of school. I'll use 'transition' to mean any significant change (planned or unplanned) within or between educational settings.

But why attend to transition? Surely children are programmed to slide effortlessly into new classrooms, make friends and bond easily with unfamiliar teachers? No, they are not. Transition can be fraught with anxiety that has a direct impact on academic performance. Pupils have to manage a very complex situation in which the formal curriculum is the least of their concerns.

There is evidence that children who fail to make a successful transition from primary to secondary school are more likely to become alienated, to truant or to create difficulties and disruptions when they are in school. Their concerns generally include these:

1   The size and more complex organisation of the new school.

2   New forms of discipline and authority.

3   New demands with regard to work.

4   Making new friends.

5   The prospect of being bullied.

A Multi-disciplinary Approach to supporting Student Transition into Higher Education: a pilot study, edited by Paul Blagburn and Sophie Cloutterbuck (student participation and transition managers), London Metropolitan University.

The Impact of School Transition and Transfers on Pupil Progress and Attainment, by Maurice Galton, John Gray and Jean Ruddock, Research Report 131 of Homerton College, Cambridge.

In *Visible Learning* (2009), John Hattie has assembled a huge number of educational studies by theme and then ranked different interventions by their impact on achievement. At the top of the list by a clear margin is pupil self-assessment. At the bottom is mobility. In fact, mobility is one of the few factors that sends pupil achievement backwards; if you move school too often without support, your grades go down.

Transition to secondary school gets most of the attention and the issues listed on the previous page are genuine. But there are other equally important moves to which the same generic thinking can be applied. Leaving your mum or dad for the first time to spend a morning at nursery is arguably more significant than going to 'big school'. Moving between infant and junior schools, getting to know a new teacher each year and then switching daily between multiple teachers in secondary education are all worthy of attention, as are moves to sixth form and going on to university.

Research carried out by London Metropolitan University suggests that roughly two-thirds of all university drop-outs happen during the first year. There is also evidence that most students make the decision to leave university within the first few weeks of that year. Effective transition and induction are fundamental in supporting students after sixth form.

The transitions above, however difficult, are planned. Unexpected transitions present even greater challenges, for example those experienced by traveller families and refugees (both international and domestic), and those presented by family upheaval, school closures and three- to two-tier restructuring. These situations all demand an equally effective approach.

A model for transition

Is there a model that describes both personal, human transitions and the wide range of planned and unplanned educational ones? Yes, there is, and it has its roots in the study of transition to secondary school:

Galton's five bridges

In 1999, Maurice Galton and colleagues looked in detail at what pupils may need to progress successfully into secondary education. They identified five areas of effective transition and expressed them using the metaphor of five bridges.

Galton argued that pupils must cross each bridge successfully, a challenge made very much easier by timely and informed intervention by Year 6 and Year 7 teachers.

The bridges fall neatly into two groups:

Social/organisational bridges

   1 Bureaucratic bridge

   2 Social and emotional bridge

   3 Curriculum bridge

Academic bridges

   4 Pedagogy bridge

   5 Management of learning bridge

Social/organisational bridges

1 The bureaucratic bridge involves formal liaison between schools, usually at senior-management level, and covers the transfer of:

- pupil records and other information;
- achievement data;
- work samples.

2 The social and emotional bridge includes development of social links between peer groups of pupils and between pupils and their caregivers within the new school before, during and after transition. It looks at:

- recognising, valuing and managing emotions;
- friendships and relationships;
- bullying and other anxieties;
- teachers' adaptation to new arrangements.

3 The curriculum bridge addresses the continuity and progression of subject matter through teacher liaison and planning for:

- cross-phase teaching;
- joint projects;
- bridging units;
- summer schools;
- joint training days;
- subject continuity.

Academic bridges

The two academic bridges get less attention that the others, but are the ones through which performance dips can be tackled.

4 The pedagogy bridge develops a shared understanding of how pupils are taught, not just of what they are taught. It considers:

- teaching skills and styles;
- teachers' perspectives on learning;
- teacher training;
- teacher exchanges between primary and secondary schools;
- cross-phase employment.

5   The management of learning bridge considers how each pupil can be encouraged to manage the transition by understanding themselves as a unique learner. It involves:

- ❍ induction;
- ❍ learner logs;
- ❍ thinking/study skills;
- ❍ learning to learn;
- ❍ learning styles;
- ❍ whole-school practice;
- ❍ orientation/inclusion activities.

Customising the model

The five bridges model is a powerful generic method for thinking about any and all transitions. Here it is stripped back into prompt questions to ask when designing or evaluating a transition programme:

Bridge 1

- ❍ What systems need to be in place to manage the transfer of information?
- ❍ What organisation and administration needs to take place?

Bridge 2

- ❍ What provision has been made for valuing emotions and expressing them appropriately?
- ❍ What provision has been made for marking the end of relationships?
- ❍ What provision has been made for building and maintaining new relationships?

Bridge 3

- ❍ What knowledge and understanding will be carried forward and further developed?

Bridge 4

- ❍ How will those involved in the process behave and offer support?
- ❍ How will those involved in the process ensure consistency of approach?

Bridge 5

- ❍ Which skills, attitudes and self-knowledge will be useful?

Try applying the model to a 3-year-old starting nursery and to an adult approaching divorce or working through a bereavement. Try asking each question for a particular transition. It *will* make sense and the answers will create an effective experience for all involved.

All things must change to something new.

Henry Wadsworth Longfellow

A programme for transition

Children experience planned and unplanned transitions within and between school years. Successful educational transition has five key elements which are shared by the non-educational ones. A child may move to secondary school and their parents may separate. Both share common features and needs.

'Nothing is as certain as change', goes the saying, and it leads to an obvious conclusion. Pupils should be formally taught about transition, rather than just receiving support through a particular one. Given the inevitability of change in their lives, we serve them well if we teach them to ask Galton's bridges questions for themselves.

Key features

Transition programmes vary with need and context, but if they are inspired by Galton's thinking then several features will emerge:

- Celebrations, rites of passage and closure events.
- Welcoming, ice-breaking, relationship-building events.
- Formal transfer of documents.
- 'Learning about change' sessions.
- 'Learning about learning' sessions.
- Learning about the systems, rituals and routines of the new school.
- Teachers visiting each others' schools.
- Teachers liaising and designing transition experiences.
- Pupils visiting their new schools.
- Appropriate before-, during- and after-transition activities.

Designing your programme

Whether you are designing from scratch or reviewing an existing programme, carry out the short audit on page 12. It includes the prompts above, combined with Galton's five bridges questions. You'll discover what you do well already and what you need to work on next.

You now have keys to unlock a fantastic transition programme. The rest of the book provides grist to your mill, but to start with there's an example of successful transition in action on the following pages (pages 13–17).

Transition programme audit and design

			Notes:
Respond to each of the prompts for your particular transition programme.			Examples of effective practice

Galton's bridges

Are systems in place to manage the transfer of information?			
Yes	No	Not sure	

Is organisation and administration effective?			
Yes	No	Not sure	

Is provision made for valuing emotions and expressing them appropriately?			
Yes	No	Not sure	

Is provision made for marking the end of relationships?			
Yes	No	Not sure	

Is provision made for building and maintaining new relationships?			
Yes	No	Not sure	

Is knowledge and understanding continuous?			
Yes	No	Not sure	

Do those involved in the process offer appropriate support?			
Yes	No	Not sure	

Do those involved in the process have a consistent approach?			
Yes	No	Not sure	

Are skills, attitudes and self-knowledge made explicit?			
Yes	No	Not sure	

Programme content

Are there celebrations, rites of passage and closure events?			
Yes	No	Not sure	

Are there welcoming, ice-breaking, relationship-building events?			
Yes	No	Not sure	

Is there a formal transfer of documents?			
Yes	No	Not sure	

Are there 'Learning about change' sessions?			
Yes	No	Not sure	

Are there 'Learning about learning' sessions?			
Yes	No	Not sure	

Do pupils learn about the systems, rituals and routines of the new school?			
Yes	No	Not sure	

Do teachers visit each other's schools?			
Yes	No	Not sure	

Do teachers liaise and design transition experiences?			
Yes	No	Not sure	

Do pupils visit their new schools?			
Yes	No	Not sure	

Are there appropriate before-, during- and after-transition activities?			
Yes	No	Not sure	

Three areas to celebrate – we do this well

1.

2.

3.

Three areas to develop – this will help us

4.

5.

6.

Action plan for 4, 5, 6:

It's in the detail: The Westgate School, Winchester

The Westgate School in Winchester is a high-achieving, mixed comprehensive for 11–16-year-olds. Year 7 pupils arrive with above average levels of achievement, and leave five years later well above average. Contributing to this success are the school's quality of teaching, whole-child provision, pastoral care and leadership, and an exemplary approach to transition.

Claire Fyvie-Rae, head of Year 7, has created a rigorous and constantly evolving programme defined equally by the needs of pupils, teachers and parents. Her method is characterised by enthusiasm, fun, attention to detail and extensive behind-the-scenes thinking, planning and evaluation.

Year on year Claire remains Year 7 head so that she can develop links with feeder primaries. The rest of the year leaders are on a four-year cycle. Claire believes this to be a unique approach and knows from experience that it works very well.

Claire's transition philosophy extends its roots down into Years 3 and 4 while reaching up and beyond Year 7. Seeking learning paybacks for the future, Claire and her transition team take the time to observe and understand every child's needs, evaluate learning behaviours and then to provide for them consistently and effectively – both during transition activities and once the school year begins.

By the time you read this, Claire will have further developed her transition package, but the sequence of events at the time of writing is shown on the following pages.

Transition over 14 months

T: transition

T–12

T–11

October (T–11 months)
Parents submit applications to local authority.

September/October (T–12 months)
Claire, headteacher, head boy and head girl visit feeder primaries:

- presentations about schools' facilities, pastoral care, subjects;
- information about timetables, extra-curricular activities, exams, uniforms;
- Q&A sessions;
- sessions customised for each primary school and open to all parents (Y3 to Y6).

T–6

T–4

March (T–6 months)
Local authority allocates places. Prospective pupils complete an 'About Myself' activity:

- hobbies, interests, personality, favourite subjects
- friends not named to avoid skewing tutor groups to primary school;
- pupils reassured 'You will be with someone from your primary school';
- used to sort Year 7 into two halves provisionally, around modern foreign languages learning.

May (T–4 months)
Claire and school counsellor visit schools sending 3+ pupils:

- informal sessions addressing worries, facilities, planner (a diary and learning organiser), uniform, etc.;
- counsellor uses juggling as a metaphor for all the new stuff to handle in Year 7.

T–2

T–3

June (T–3 months)
Taster day including session with counsellor and subject teachers.
Additional visits for those who need to see the school in a smaller group or again.

Early July (T–2 months)
Induction evening for pupils and their parents held in school:

- tutor groups revealed;
- children and parents separate;
- children meet their tutor;
- parents attend parallel sessions run by senior language teacher on rules, parent partnership, etc.

T+1

T–0

October (T+1month)
Meet the tutor:

– tutors off timetable for the day;
– two-way information-sharing
  between tutors and parents;
– Year 7 and 8 homework evening;
– parents' debrief session – feedback
  worked into next year's provision.

September (T–0 months)
New school year begins:

– first day;
– Year 7 zoned play area.

November (T+2 months)
Primary headteacher visits – optional part of
the programme:

– selected pupils are shadowed by their
  ex-headteacher;
– headteachers further enabled to inform
  their own pupils about life at Westgate.

T–2

T+2

Late July (T–2 months)
Claire runs a one- to two-week optional summer camp
that has at least 76% uptake:

– staff-run activities: fun, inclusive, team building;
– pupils write daily diaries;
– teachers use time to observe and plan for pupils' pastoral
  learning needs;
– daily staff debrief sessions and nightly requests for
  parents' feedback;
– last-day barbecue for staff, children and parents;
– assisted places available through social services;
– pupils with child and adolescent mental health and
  other service involvement observed carefully and
  nurtured/supported appropriately during the camp.

The information gathered during summer camp is
compiled and sent to tutors in preparation for September.
It provides a working knowledge of each child – their
needs, strengths and likely provision.

It also gives a heads-up to the school counsellor, who will
customise intervention for the coming year. For example,
information from Westgate's 2011 cohort prompted him
to run a bereavement group, a divorce group and a young
carers' group.

Outreach and engagement

Claire extends her activities beyond this set sequence. She is developing The Westgate School's public image as a school that reaches out to primary-school children (both within and beyond the catchment) in order to share its excitement for learning in specific subject areas.

Championing its science specialism, The Westgate School organises events such as mad scientist lectures and hands-on laboratory days. It runs a sports festival, role-play journalism, a Year 5 production and ICT days in which Year 4 and 5 pupils make films and create DVDs. A powerful by-product has been the transfer of ICT skills from secondary specialists to primary teachers via their young pupils.

Mathematics, science, drama, English, modern foreign languages, PE and humanities all contribute to outreach and engagement programmes. The Westgate School holds open mornings that regularly host over a hundred parents and attract children from schools from which there has been no previous attendance. Any and all contact of this nature between The Westgate School and its potential pupils (and their parents) eases transition anxieties and accelerates engagement with learning once pupils begin in Year 7.

Pupils' opinions

With such a fine example of transition available, I was interested to know how it impacted on pupils and their achievement. I have a theory that the quality of transition – its success in leading pupils across Galton's bridges – will relate not only to pupil well-being but also to their enjoyment of learning and ultimately their grades.

This is tricky to prove as the impact of transition may become lost in the noise as pupils progress through the school. But I made a start by interviewing 18 students from Year 7 to Year 10. I was interested in their opinions about summer camp and how it affected their learning and potential performance in GCSE:

Summer camp will generally affect your grades. If you've done transition you get rid of all that worrying and if you're in lessons worrying it kind of brings you off subject and you don't really get much of the learning done. You focus on tasks more. Summer camp gives you more confidence.

Summer camp's a really good idea because you can get used to the school building and you can make new friends earlier and you can get used to the way the school's run. Also because you're less anxious, because you've already made many of your new friends before you start, it makes you concentrate more on your learning. You're less hassled to get to your lessons.

Summer camp's a really great idea because you get to know the school before you even start. You can come from primary really nervous but if you come to summer camp you really understand the school. It just releases all the strain. When you're in your lessons that year then you know you've already made your friends and you're less anxious.

Just 'cause you've settled in doesn't mean it's going to affect your grades in any way. It might help you in Year 7 but by the time you get to Year 11 you already have that confidence in you from other years.

I don't believe that summer camp affects your outcomes at GCSE at all although I do believe it might have a small impression. It's not portraying the school as it will be.

Summer camp makes a good impression for new students but it could have a negative effect if you got into the wrong friendship group. Even with this I don't think it [summer camp influence] would stretch to GCSE results. For most people you generally get friends and find the right group and that helps your learning. It helped me in the first year or so.

I believe that summer camp has a negative impact on GCSE results because if you have your first impression of the school as being a sort of matey place to be and all the staff are like your friends and it's really a comfortable place to be then I think that has a bad effect on your GCSEs. I think being comfortable means you'll be more likely not to be motivated.

Summer camp is a really positive experience. It's debatable if that helps you academically with your GCSEs because that really does depend on what kind of person you are. I think any detrimental effects of not going to summer camp would be negated by the time you get to your GCSEs.

I think that summer camp does help GCSE results but not in such a direct way. So if you enjoy summer camp you're going to enjoy school more in the first year, you're going to make friends and focus on studies straight away and enjoy subjects straight away and carry on enjoying them throughout to Year 11 and then hopefully GCSE results should come easily. The teachers are quite friendly then, you're not going to be motivated, you won't take them seriously, that's why pupils in Years 10 and 11 should be able to run summer camp.

These opinions are honest, varied and genuine, and provide invaluable feedback to Claire and her team for the programme's continuing evolution. The purpose of a transition programme like this one is not initially to raise test scores, but to support pupils as they move between educational contexts. However, ultimately we would expect some traceable yet indirect impact on learning outcomes.

Section 2
Learning

All about learners

When pupils move between classes and schools, they don't suddenly and magically adapt to a new set of requirements and expectations. They need time to learn and time to acclimatise. However, each child does bring with them a unique set of learning skills, a set of specific talents and an inherent flexibility to adjust to new situations. These characteristics remain constant throughout the change and a deeper knowledge of them will inform our transition plans.

An evolving brain and mind

School transitions generally coincide with developmental stages, not least around the age of 11–12. Moving to secondary school overlaps with one of the most turbulent times that a human being faces: the anatomical one of the onset of puberty. Hurray! Not only do we ask children to de-camp, uproot and move on; we ask them to do it while they have little or no control over the hormones charging around their bodies. Throw a wild card of family upheaval or friendship issues into the pot and we have a potent mix.

A little understanding here will go a long way.

At puberty children become biologically able to reproduce, develop mature reproductive organs and manifest a frightening array of secondary sexual characteristics such as breasts, beards and deep voices. Puberty involves a growth spurt, and changes in height and weight, the heart and lungs, and especially the brain.

The brain goes through many stages of development, influenced by both genes and environment. It grows in an ordered way, but not at a steady pace. Functions come on line and brain areas mature according to a set pattern, but there are key moments when growth speeds up. What happens at these times is critical, and can have major implications for future learning, interests, attitudes and eventual life success.

One critical time occurs just before and just into puberty. If we know what's going on we can plan for it.

Brain growth has two features: an increase in the number of brain cells (neurons, the grey matter) and a strengthening of the long-range connections between them (myelin-coated fibres, the white stuff). Up until about 18 months of age, a baby's brain overproduces grey matter, which is then shaped by external stimuli, rather like a block of stone being carved into a statue. The quantity and quality of the baby's experience determine how its brain turns out.

Nothing endures but change.

Heraclitus

But there is a second similar period of grey matter overproduction just before puberty, just around transition.

This major growth spurt has implications in several important areas: personality, emotion and language.

Personality

The blooming of grey matter is centred in the frontal lobes, a part of the brain associated with personality and high-level thinking skills such as planning, reasoning, discernment, judgement and impulse control. While this area is being sculpted by experiences, a child may act irrationally, impulsively, unpredictably and without apparent forethought. There may be swings between extremes of behaviour and mood with no obvious trigger. Although this may be a demanding time for parents, teachers and the children themselves, it is some comfort that such difficulties are normal, natural and explainable by science. And out of the neuro-turmoil, a unique and stable personality will usually emerge.

Emotions

While the pre-frontal cortex is emerging into its final adult shape, it is less able to discern the nuances of emotion in others. It may have a hard time discriminating between, say, an angry face and a fearful one. Children's ability to recognise emotion in others, based on facial expression, lessens as they pass 11 and 12 years of age. They tend to register emotion predominantly in the amygdala, the area of the brain that responds first to visual stimuli. But they do not then follow this up with accurate reasoned thought in the pre-frontal cortex, as an older person would. This may lead to difficulty in reading non-verbal signals and acting appropriately.

Language

All changes, even the most longed for, have their melancholy.

Anatole France

The growth of white matter begins in the front of the brain and moves in a wave backwards, tailing off quickly after the age of 12. This growth features a surge of development in areas dedicated to language. Researchers have linked it to a critical period for learning two aspects of not only the first language but also of a second language: grammar and accent. However, other features (vocabulary and semantics) are not similarly restricted to this window of opportunity and can be learned just as easily after the age of 12 as before.

Learners at transfer

So much is changing in the educational life of children at transfer – never mind what may be happening outside school. The last thing they really need is such mammoth changes inside their heads and their bodies. But if teachers choose to be guided by the findings of neuroscience, they can go some way to making learning experiences more appropriate and supportive. Remember, the following are not excuses for challenging behaviour, but they are perfectly plausible reasons for it:

○ Children's personalities and sense of self are a flexible, dynamic and volatile work in progress, strongly and unpredictably influenced by day-to-day experience.

○ Children's higher-order thinking skills are erratic and developing.

○ Children's ability to recognise emotions in others accurately is temporarily impaired.

○ Children's ability to learn certain aspects of languages (particularly grammar and accent) reduces sharply at puberty.

All about learning

Our ever-expanding knowledge of the inner workings of the brain sheds some light on the development of the learning process and the uniqueness of each pupil. What we do with this knowledge at transition is another matter.

Styles and success

Each pupil is different from all the rest. Their styles of learning and their expectations of teaching do not change between classes and schools. We should give time to understanding the diversity before us and to exploit it in the design of lessons.

Academics continue to debate the research surrounding thinking skills, learning styles and multiple intelligences, but wherever we stand on these issues they do provide us with an effective framework for thinking about learning.

Creating a Personal Learning Profile is a wholly appropriate activity for transition. It confirms and celebrates learning to date and provides signposts for the future.

Here are three bites at the same cherry: a multiple intelligences profile, a thinking styles profile and a learning styles profile. Our thinking style reveals how we approach problem solving and how we best contribute in a group or team. Like multiple intelligences, this is not a label or a limit that relates to a single style, but rather a preferred approach plus a mix of potential strengths that come into play with the demands of different situations.

Use the results of this profile individually or in combination to help pupils cross Galton's first and fifth bridges: the profile is a valuable document to be sent between schools, and useful communication of learning expectations.

Multiple intelligences: How am I clever? How can I best succeed?

Give each prompt a score between 0 and 3; 3 means you agree with it a lot; 0 not at all. Add up the scores for each intelligence and identify your three strongest ones. The chances are that you'll prefer subjects and activities involving these. Now identify your two weakest intelligences. You'll probably avoid these if you can, and if that's not possible you'll not enjoy them as much as the other three.

WORDS

I enjoy reading and writing.	0 1 2 3			
I enjoy listening and speaking.	0 1 2 3			
I can talk my way out of trouble.	0 1 2 3			
I can persuade people to do things.	0 1 2 3			
I get into trouble at school for talking too much.	0 1 2 3	Total:	

LOGIC

I can do maths in my head easily.	0 1 2 3			
I get into trouble at school for arguing a point.	0 1 2 3			
I enjoy playing games that require me to think.	0 1 2 3			
I like to have reasons for things.	0 1 2 3			
I like to plan ahead.	0 1 2 3	Total:	

PICTURES

I can picture things in my head easily.	0 1 2 3			
I enjoy doing art and watching films.	0 1 2 3			
I am good at following maps.	0 1 2 3			
I like to draw or doodle.	0 1 2 3			
I get into trouble at school for daydreaming.	0 1 2 3	Total:	

BODY

I enjoy sport and physical activity.	0 1 2 3			
I like making and fixing things.	0 1 2 3			
I get into trouble at school for not sitting still.	0 1 2 3			
I need to touch things to learn more about them.	0 1 2 3			
I use my hands and arms when I talk.	0 1 2 3	Total:	

MUSIC

I like singing.	0 1 2 3			
I tap my fingers/feet when I hear music.	0 1 2 3			
I listen to music a lot.	0 1 2 3			
I can hear music in my head.	0 1 2 3			
I hum/sing while I'm working.	0 1 2 3	Total:	

Personal Learning Profile 2

Multiple intelligences (continued)

PEOPLE

I am good at working out how other people feel.	0	1	2	3	
I like working in a team.	0	1	2	3	
When I have a problem, I ask someone for help.	0	1	2	3	
I know what makes people tick.	0	1	2	3	
I like to go out.	0	1	2	3	Total:

SELF

I like working on my own.	0	1	2	3	
I enjoy my own company.	0	1	2	3	
I know what I'm good at.	0	1	2	3	
I know what I want to do with my life.	0	1	2	3	
When I have a problem, I sort it out myself.	0	1	2	3	Total:

NATURE

I enjoy spending time outside.	0	1	2	3	
I can name many plants/animals.	0	1	2	3	
I enjoy being in a garden or wood/forest.	0	1	2	3	
I can name clouds/star constellations.	0	1	2	3	
My family keeps a pet and I enjoy caring for it.	0	1	2	3	Total:

LIFE

I am part of a religious group and take part in worship.	0	1	2	3	
I can meditate.	0	1	2	3	
I am interested in big questions about life.	0	1	2	3	
I pray now and again.	0	1	2	3	
I believe in a power beyond our understanding.	0	1	2	3	Total:

Personal Learning Profile 3

*Your **thinking style** shows how you approach problem solving and the role you prefer in a group team.*

*Rank the four possible responses to each prompt below. The one **MOST** like you scores **4**. The one **LEAST** like you scores **1**. The first section is an example.*

At school I most value:		
a	how others feel	*1*
b	creativity	*4*
c	getting the work done	*3*
d	planning how I spend my time.	*2*

1. At school I most value:		
a	how others feel	
b	creativity	
c	getting the job done	
d	planning and systems.	

2. When the learning gets difficult I:		
a	organise things	
b	focus on getting the work finished	
c	focus on how I'm feeling	
d	think about new ways of getting it done.	

3. My strength in a group is to:		
a	work hard and finish things	
b	have ideas	
c	get on well with others	
d	use my common sense.	

4. I'm most proud of my:		
a	care for others	
b	flexibility	
c	success	
d	efficiency.	

5. Others would say that I am		
a	not reliable	
b	too sensitive	
c	impatient	
d	bossy.	

6. I prefer to learn with people (classmates or teachers) who:		
a	like to discover things	
b	like things to run smoothly	
c	get on well with others	
d	solve problems quickly.	

Thinking style (continued)

7. At school I'm happiest when:		
a	my planning gets results	
b	I get freedom to explore my ideas and interests	
c	the work gets done without wasting time	
d	people trust me and rely on me.	

8. During a crisis I:		
a	make sure everyone understands what's going on	
b	stay positive and enjoy the challenge	
c	accept responsibility and act	
d	stick to the plan and hold tight.	

9. My teachers most probably see me as a:		
a	team player	
b	risk taker	
c	hard worker	
d	good organiser.	

10. People solve problems best when they:		
a	think logically	
b	work together	
c	seek new solutions	
d	use trial and error.	

Transfer your ranking scores to this table, then add up the numbers in each column and enter the totals at the bottom.

Question	C	E	S	R
1	b =	a =	d =	c =
2	d =	c =	a =	b =
3	b =	c =	d =	a =
4	b =	a =	d =	c =
5	a =	b =	d =	c =
6	a =	c =	b =	d =
7	b =	d =	a =	c =
8	b =	a =	d =	c =
9	b =	a =	d =	c =
10	c =	b =	d =	a =
Total				

Thinking style (continued)

Mark your total score for each of the four statements on the chart below and join up the four points. This shape represents your balance of styles – Creative, Emotional, Systems, Results.

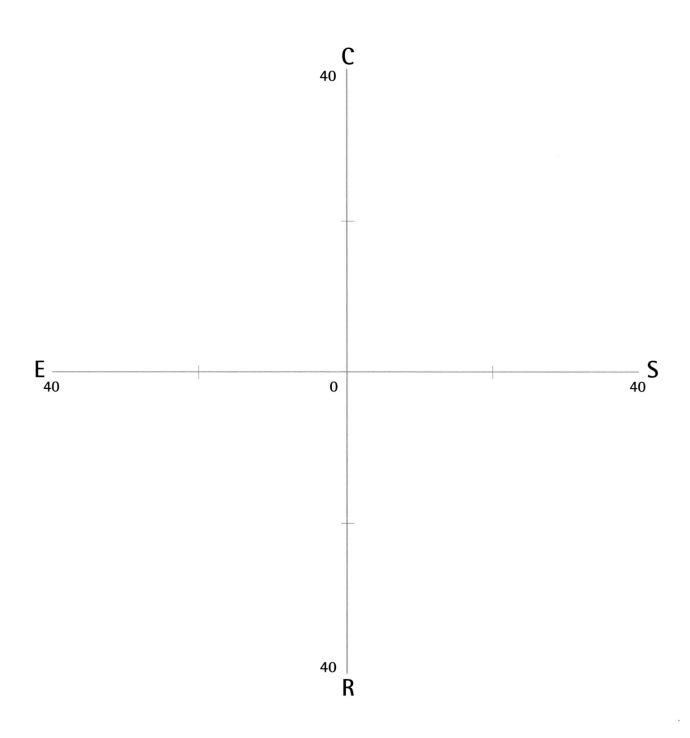

Personal Learning Profile 6

*Your **learning style** shows how you like to work and learn.*
Imagine that you are learning something new.

Where

Do you prefer (tick up to 4 boxes):

- ☐ noise in the background (e.g. music/TV)
- ☐ silence
- ☐ bright light
- ☐ dim or soft light
- ☐ hot room
- ☐ warm room
- ☐ cool room
- ☐ cold room
- ☐ outside for some of the time (weather permitting)
- ☐ other.

Do you prefer to (tick up to 3 boxes):

- ☐ sit at a desk
- ☐ sit in a comfy chair
- ☐ lay down on the floor / a bean-bag
- ☐ get up and move about from time to time
- ☐ stay still in one place
- ☐ eat (have snacks) as you work
- ☐ other.

When

Do you prefer to learn (tick up to 3 boxes):

- ☐ early morning
- ☐ mid-morning
- ☐ afternoon
- ☐ early evening
- ☐ late evening
- ☐ night
- ☐ other.

Getting started, keeping going

Do you (tick up to 3 boxes):

- ☐ find it is easy to start
- ☐ need external pressure (e.g. a deadline)
- ☐ continue with a task until it's done
- ☐ tackle several jobs at once
- ☐ become easily distracted by other things?
- ☐ other.

How

When you are learning, do you prefer (tick up to 8 boxes):

- ☐ routine, regular tasks
- ☐ variety of demands
- ☐ learning in small steps
- ☐ getting the 'big picture' first
- ☐ time to reflect
- ☐ working alone
- ☐ working in pairs
- ☐ working in a team
- ☐ reading
- ☐ listening
- ☐ seeing (e.g. demonstration)
- ☐ having a go yourself
- ☐ talking to others
- ☐ self-talk
- ☐ writing
- ☐ doodling
- ☐ fiddle
- ☐ other.

All about teaching

Your own teaching style emerges from a combination of your experience as a pupil, your initial and ongoing training, the nature of your pupils, the character of your classes, the demands of your subjects and your day-to-day moods.

Primary teaching is usually delivered by an individual generalist, secondary by multiple specialists. Some schools preserve aspects of the primary approach into Year 7 – and sometimes beyond – using integrated curricula. Others make a clean break. Galton argues for a certain level of 'discontinuity' at transition so pupils know they've moved school.

Skills and growth

You'll have some flexibility in style: a repertoire of approaches and an arena in which you can operate. But there will be limits. Have a go at the Personal Learning Profile yourself. Quietly. After the feathers and sequins from taster day have been swept away. Then take a look at who's on their way up to you or who's leaving. Is there a style conflict? Do you and your colleagues have the capacity to accommodate all pupils' learning preferences?

My education was dismal. I went to a series of schools for mentally disturbed teachers.

Woody Allen

Whatever age group is coming or going, you can use the Personal Learning Profile not only to reveal individual needs, but to define the nature of whole teaching groups. Yes, it's an effort to add up and average all those scores, but it's effort with significant payback. Imagine knowing that one particular class will respond more eagerly to interpersonal, self-motivated tasks involving a clear process and opportunities for creativity. Or that another class might rebel if you try group work outside. Personal Learning Profiles can accelerate your working knowledge of pupils and ease their transition between the styles of teaching in different schools.

Section 3
Leading

How to lead transition

Transition programmes are usually initiated and led by individuals and teams based in the destination school. They rely on the cooperation and engagement of teachers in feeder schools. An effective transition programme is mutually beneficial and lends itself to collaborative rather than didactic leadership. However, someone will have to take responsibility for its success and they will need the right mix of influence and power to do that.

Leadership style

The leadership and management of successful transition is characterised by clear forward planning, attention to detail, effective communication and frequent, timely liaison between teachers. A touch of flair and dazzle is also needed when it comes to designing exciting transition events, plus a good deal of sensitivity to the various needs of children and their parents. Oh, and you'll also want a good dose of charisma to inspire others to join you on your quest for the ultimate transition experience.

Don't worry at all if you're lacking in some or most of these domains: the leadership quality that trumps all others is the ability to know your strengths and to delegate appropriately. Carry out a quick self-assessment, then find your team:

Skill/Attribute	Can do it/Have it	Can get by	Find someone
Forward planning			
Attention to detail			
Communication			
Teacher liaison			
Creative			
Sensitive			
Charismatic			

Involving parents and teachers

Parents seek information and reassurance about the transition process, together with advice for supporting their children during the transition period. Schools can help with both requests. Well-crafted letters providing basic information and written with empathy, combined with professionally friendly meetings and open days, will go a long way towards getting parents on board and keeping them there.

'We fully understand that transition can be an anxious time for you and your child. This is perfectly normal. We'll do our best to answer any questions you may have and to provide all the information you'll need.'

Involving your colleagues may need a 'What's in it for me?' approach, relying on the strength of your school's professional learning community and senior leadership. It would be wise not to underestimate the size of a transition leadership task. Ensure that you have the support you need up front.

How to communicate between schools

Communication within and between schools is essential for transition success. Remember that responsibility for the communicated message does not lie solely with the person receiving it. Just because you've spoken, that does not guarantee that you have been heard or understood. Communication is a shared obligation. If communications are preserved and encourage interaction, then understanding is more likely. A Wikispace provides a free and effective method of achieving this.

Wikispace video projects

Imagine a blank mini Wikipedia just waiting for you to fill it up with your own content – text, video, audio, links, blogs, comments and discussion. Well, imagine no more. You'll easily get one at http://www.wikispaces.com. It's free for educational users, and after joining up you're less than a minute away from creating your very own space.

Here's one I made earlier: http://lsbu60secondwiki.wikispaces.com/ I created it in early 2012 with student ambassadors from London South Bank University (LSBU). Its purpose is to inform and inspire sixth-formers as they decide what to do after A Levels. But it also functions as a transition support resource when these students move not just to LSBU but on to any university or college. They can access it wherever they end up and can continue to contribute.

The short videos are intentionally raw and genuine. The last thing I wanted was gloss and polish. Teenagers today can sniff out spin at 1,000 metres, so it's best to tell it as it is. The advice is relevant and accurate and given by university students who are not long out of sixth form themselves.

The resource is currently in use by several schools in south London and offers a model that can be repeated for any transition: there is a space for sixth-formers created by university students, one for Year 11s made by sixth-formers, another for Year 6s created by Year 7s, and one for Year 2s filmed by Year 3s.

Here is the task design I used at LSBU. It's easily copied and customised for other years, groups and purposes:

The 60-second Wiki-learning challenge

Your task in a small group is to produce twenty 60-second videos for a university-learning Wikispace. The videos must concisely and accurately inform viewers about specific aspects of learning, studying, aspiration and success – both in the university and beyond. You will be able to choose some, but not all, of the content.

You will have up to three hours' planning time supported by a learning consultant, followed by a week in which you can do further preparation if you want. The learning consultant will return after a week and be available for a day to film your work. Your videos will be uploaded shortly afterwards.

The Wikispace will be online with full public access. However, the target audience is Year 12 and 13 students who aspire to attend university or who want support during their transition to university.

This is a great opportunity to work creatively, under time pressure, both in a small team and individually. It will also be an opportunity for you to showcase effective verbal and visual communication skills and to clarify your own understanding of the content expressed in the videos.

Acceptance for this short project implies your permission to use videos recorded as described above.

TASK 1
Each individual is required to prepare a personal 60-second biography for filming. This must include your name, age, course, motivation and aspirations, and one piece of advice aimed at sixth-formers.

TASK 2
Your team is required to prepare around twenty 60-second presentations for filming. Between you, you need to share out the topics below. The learning consultant will provide input on concepts with which you are not familiar or about which you have questions.

* Is there a correct path to university?
* How to choose the right subject and course.
* How to cope under pressure.
* What university can do for me.
* Overcoming my fears.
* How do you overcome difficulties?
* What made you choose to come to university?
* What's the best thing about university?
* Where can you go for advice and learning support?
* How do you manage your money?
* What is 'learning style'?
* How to find out your preferred studying style.
* How to manage your time well.
* What is 'mindset?'
* How to use your mindset.

Students add their own ideas to the list.

The videos may be set in any reasonable and appropriate location and may take any form that supports the message and does not involve extra expense such as CGI resources or Oscar-nominated actors. During the week of preparation questions may be mailed to mike@thinkingclassroom.co.uk. It's expected that you will take no more than an hour of your time preparing your work for filming day. Thank you for doing this. Your time is a gift to younger learners.

Using the internet and mobiles

As well as sharing responsibility for the message, offer flexibility in the medium and method of communication. Contacting parents may be far more effective via bulk text or well-timed email than in any other way, and likewise pupils can be kept informed via their mobile phones. Before you object, hear two things:

1 'Schools normally react to technological change by confiscating it to protect the past: ballpoint pens to save our handwriting, calculators to save our arithmetic, digital watches to save our analogue timekeeping, mobile phones to save our … er well, just because they are new' (Stephen Heppell)

2 Some schools turn mobile phones to their advantage and apply them to learning. They accept the inevitability that pupils will own and use them. So they set a minimum specification and outline how the phones are expected to be used in class. For example, 'You'll need a camera to record the equipment set-up and results in science so that you can write up the experiment accurately.' Or 'You'll need some form of voice record to make notes on the poem for next lesson.'

Not convinced? Try 3.

3 I recently visited my favourite running website: www.mapmyrun.com. It invited me to try its new beta version and presented just two options to click:

    a) Try it now.
    b) I hate change.

How to manage emotions and relationships

Leading transition (or leading anything for that matter) demands a high level of emotional intelligence). You need the skills to recognise your own emotions and the wherewithal to express them appropriately. You need self-motivation and trust. You also need a certain talent for building and maintaining relationships with children, their parents and teachers from other schools.

With all this in order you'll be well placed to model emotional intelligence to children and suitably enthused to include activities about managing feelings and building relationships in your transition programme. The lessons in Part 4 are infused with opportunities to do just that.

Friends and fears

Pupils may have strong but contradictory feelings about transition. They may feel both excited and fearful: full of dread one minute, then brimming with optimism the next. We must reassure them that this is normal – not necessarily easy, but to be fully expected.

For example, moving to secondary school raises significant feelings about loss and change, vulnerability, belonging and feeling safe. Transition may threaten the foundations of the self that a child has carefully built during previous years. It's therefore important to acknowledge how each learner is or might be feeling

Professor Stephen Heppell is an internationally respected leader in learning, media and new technologies.

You know that
children are growing
up when they start
asking questions that
have answers.

John J. Plomp

without judging or trying to 'fix things' – whatever their age or the transition they face. Responding with 'Don't worry; it'll be all right' is probably the worst thing we can say at this point. They'll be far better off if you say something like this: 'It's not easy, is it? I know how this feels – all mixed up. Well, that's OK. Tricky, new, but still OK and as it should be. Lots of folk feel like this too.' A response like this validates and values their feelings without trying to hurry them along to 'feeling better'.

Talking, writing and other forms of expression should be used when feelings need a voice. Here's a prompt grid to help structure emotional expression.

Let learners choose one element from each column as appropriate. For example, I want to express *Feeling mixed up* by *Painting*. Then give them the opportunity to try what happens when they do that. If one combination doesn't work, encourage them to select another and try that method.

I want to express	by
Fear	Writing a poem
Dread	Painting
Feeling mixed up	Making a clay model
Excitement	Talking to a friend
Optimism	Writing a song
Melancholy	Writing a diary

Bullying and bravery

A lot of bullying is imagined, but some is very real and it is a clear and present danger for children at transition. A school without bullying is a school without human beings because bullying is one of the inevitable and bleaker aspects of our flawed natures. However, a school that fails to act to reduce bullying or to respond swiftly to its occurrence is itself inhuman.

Bullying is the intentional and repeated harming of another person who does not have the capacity to retaliate. A one-off playground fight is not bullying. Regular tripping in the corridor and theft of lunch money is. Children need to be clear about which is which and to report incidents accurately.

But it's a brave victim who can report such intimidation, especially under threat of further physical or verbal violence. One of the most emotionally intelligent methods for dealing with bullying is the 'no blame' approach. It has its fans and it has its critics. Decide on its value for yourself.

The no blame philosophy rests on the premise the bullies behave as they do because they too have been or are being bullied. Chastisement and punishment will do little to change their behavior, whereas confronting them with their actions may.

Young people are in a condition like permanent intoxication, because youth is sweet and they are growing.

Aristotle

In a teacher- or mentor-managed no blame session the victim is asked to express exactly what has been happening, how they feel because of it and how it has affected them. This can be written, recorded or drawn. The victim is then asked for permission to share the account directly with the bully, either in person or via an advocate.

The bully hears the account and is asked to respond. Faced with this truth and confronted by the consequences of their actions, the bully has the opportunity to apologise (face to face or through the advocate) and to change their ways without fear of punishment. The situation is then monitored.

It is essential that the bully hears how the victim has been made to feel. It's easy to debate the facts of an incident but it's a brave person who denies someone else the accurate self-reporting of their own feelings.

Of course, if the issue starts up again more serious action must be taken, especially where pupil safety is of concern. 'No blame' is intended to run parallel to existing school behaviour-management systems. It is not a replacement for rules and sanctions. 'No blame' and similar approaches offer a longer, harder road that may provide a longer-term solution rather than a quick, impermanent fix.

The real work here is in creating a school culture that gets victims and bullies into a reconciliation process. Raising awareness of bullying and offering safe places with trust and confidentiality is the key.

* * *

To finish this section we'll look at an impact study from Hailsham that demonstrates aspects of effective transition leadership and management. Hailsham is a small but rapidly growing market town of approximately 20,000 people in East Sussex. Hailsham Community College (HCC) is the only secondary school in the town and is fed by four main primaries, of which White House Primary School is one. It is unusual for White House pupils to move on to any other secondary school.

Year 6 pupils from five or six other small village primary schools also go on to HCC. Those who are not heading for Hailsham Community College are provided for by their own schools, who set up their own transition programmes.

Impact study: Hailsham Community College and White House Primary School, Hailsham

An early start: transition in Hailsham

The final week of Year 6 is a mixed blessing. It's an important rite of passage brimming with tears, anxieties, performances, discos, signed T-shirts and relaxed rules. It's also an academic wasteland in which the formal curriculum ceases to exist, displays come down and trays are emptied. What if this week switched to secondary school? What if Year 6 pupils left early to experience their first week of Year 7 before the summer holidays? Would there be a payback – a social and learning advantage? Would pupils hit the ground running come September?

Gareth Jones, advanced skills teacher and transition manager at Hailsham Community College (HCC) wanted to find out. Inspired by similar approaches in other regions, he carefully researched the concept, then invested a phenomenal amount of time and effort into the 2011 launch:

In order to make the most of this opportunity a number of arrangements had to be made much earlier than normal – specifically, house placements, assigning Year 6 students to mentor groups, and constructing teaching groups before the SATs results were available. We also needed to construct a timetable for the week that reflected our decision to dripfeed new experiences to the students and also meet the needs of Year 6 staff and HHC staff who would be delivering it.

Gareth realised that the project's success would rest in the detail. He was meticulous about considering all administrational issues – not least lunch, internet and network access, registration and uniform:

It was decided that pupils should wear their primary uniform without the sweatshirts and logos. In actual fact there was a creep in to HCC uniform during the week by their choice.

Helen Riddall is Year 6 leader at White House Primary, a feeder school to HCC:

When this was first suggested it was met with mixed reactions. Some parents thought it was a great idea – a way of ensuring children were less anxious over the summer holidays about moving on to secondary school. Some, however, thought it was a shame that the children were missing out on their last week as primary-school pupils.

I was on the fence. I could see both sides. The children would get to know their new teachers and mentor groups early and have less anxiety about getting lost and so on. But as a Year 6 teacher I initially thought it was a shame to make the change. I felt the children deserved a rite of passage from primary school and that the last week was always emotional and full of reflection on their primary career.

Most parents were on board and it went ahead. The children were much the same. Some were unhappy as they wanted to stay at primary school for as long as possible, but some – as soon as SATs were over and done with – were completely and utterly ready to move on! From a teacher's point of view, logistically it was tricky. I have a Year 5/6 class and myself and my TA were expected to go to HCC for the first two days of the transition week. Therefore, we had to arrange cover for my Year 5s.

Gareth's thorough planning of the five days involved a gradual alignment with the actual HHC school day, high-quality bespoke activities, extensive support from a group of trusty Year 7s and a careful phasing out of primary teacher presence.

On day 1 students were brought from their primary schools, arriving later than normal at 9.30. They spent the day mostly in their Year 6 classes accompanied by their Year 6 teachers and a team of Year 7 students who went to the same primary school. On day 2 they arrived under their own steam at 8.50 (five minutes after the official HCC start time) and made their way to mentor rooms. On the third day all students arrived and left with the rest of the school.

Within the early-transition week, myself and my TA went with the children to HCC. We spent Monday with the children and I actually taught a thinking skills lesson. For the rest of the day the children took part in activities around the school and sample lessons. On Tuesday the children had a full day of lessons and myself and my TA were there only as support. On the Wednesday through Friday the children were fully integrated into HCC without us, completing lessons and starting the day in their mentor groups. On the Friday, myself and my headteacher Heather Baldwin went to HCC to meet with the children to hear their points of view. All the children were very positive about the experience.

Early transition offers pupils a smooth and effective start to secondary education. It's a radical yet obvious alternative to the traditional process and needs exhaustive planning and careful leadership. The contemplation of change and the passage over Galton's five bridges is accelerated into a single week, rather than being drawn out across an anxious summer.

In September I spoke with the children about whether early transition had helped. Ninety-nine per cent of the children said it did. Parents were extremely happy and I had no negative feedback from any of the parents whose children went to HCC. The early-transition week was successful. The children gained from making that step early. I believe it helped the secondary school most as the children settled quickly in September. From a primary perspective it took work to sort things out, making sure that other classes were covered and end-of-year productions moved a week early.

Having worked closely with all involved throughout the week, I am absolutely convinced of its worth. The feedback from staff and children was excellent and every Year 6 pupil I spoke to told me how much they had enjoyed the week and how relaxed they now felt about September.

A year down the line and, in anticipation of his second early-transition event, Gareth remains fully committed to the process:

Last year we offered it to the whole Year 6 cohort, even those going to schools other than HCC, but that had limited success so this year it's only our pupils. This allows the primaries to plan for their needs more effectively.

Year 6 teachers will only be there on the first morning because feedback from this year's Year 7 [the first early-transition group] suggested that this would have been fine.

In summary:

We have had a very successful and settled year requiring virtually no changes to Year 7 teaching groups or mentor groups, which is unusual. This is mainly because, as a part of the early-transition process, we consulted time and again with the Year 6 staff, who knew the cohort best.

Section 4
Lessons

Here are 15 generic activities to add to your transition programme. They are presented in three sections for use before, during and after transition. Each one is described and then adapted (where possible) to five different types of transition:

- ❏ Starting school.
- ❏ Moving year groups.
- ❏ Moving to secondary school.
- ❏ Unexpected moves.
- ❏ Starting college/university – leaving home.

These and other generic activities support successful transition because they focus on the *how* of learning as well as the *what*. For example, if Year 6 pupils are acquainted with 'Video questions' (on page 45), then a similar activity encountered in Year 7 (with different content) will be familiar to them. They will be able to give their full attention to the new *what* because they already know the *how* – 'Hey, we did it like this at primary!'

Activities for before transition

Dream bottles

Summary:
A fairytale-style story about success, failure, dreams and decision-making, followed by a series of prompts for whole-class discussion.

Activity:
Tell this story in a way with which you are comfortable:

Once there was a boy who lived in the forest with his father. They went everywhere together and little by little the father taught his son everything he knew. He showed the boy how to fell a tree, how to catch a rabbit, how to cook a pigeon and how to repair their cottage roof. They were best friends and shared an unspoken respect for each other.

But one day a lady with emerald eyes came to the forest. The father took one look at her and fell in love. She had a stone heart and a cruel mouth, but the father saw none of this. He was enchanted by her gaze. The boy tried to warn him but the father just shooed him away. Eventually the lady allowed herself to be loved and came to live with them.

She offered the boy none of the smiles and encouragement that a mother might. Instead he shrivelled under her constant disapproval. The lady forced herself between him and his father until one day the boy was completely forgotten by his parent.

He packed his few things and left. The father and the lady saw him go but neither noticed his tears; the father was consumed by love for the lady, and she was hardened by her selfishness.

The boy wandered deeper and deeper into the forest into places where only a finger-thick beam of sunlight could break through the ancient trees. He pushed past leaves and branches never before touched by human hands. He disturbed creatures unfamiliar with his form, which scuttled away to shield their young.

Eventually the boy emerged from the trees into a clearing that surrounded a still, clear pool. Standing by the edge of the water was a deer. The animal was alert and turned its head confidently as the boy approached. He reached out to touch the deer's head and as he did words formed in his mind.

'Look into the water, reach in and take what you find.'

The boy stepped into the pool and saw two small bottles just below the surface, identical in shape and size. He dipped his hand into the water and picked them out. He held them up to the light that filled the clearing and noticed that both bottles contained golden liquid.

'Drink from one,' said the deer, 'and all your dreams will come true. You will succeed in everything you try. Drink from the other and all your dreams will wither. You will fail at everything you try. The moment you choose one bottle, the other will disappear.'

'But how do I know which one is which?' asked the boy.

When he looked up the deer had gone. He sat for a time by the pool in the clearing, thinking about his father, the cruel lady and the choice he held in his hands. Eventually he pulled the stopper from one of the bottles and drank its golden liquid.

Lead the class in discussion and debate, using questions selected from the following:

- What happened in the story?
- Which event in the story was the most significant to you?
- Why did the father reject the boy?
- How did the boy make his bottle choice – what might have been going on in his mind?
- How else could the boy have acted at the end of the story?

- What might be the consequences of choosing the 'succeed' bottle?
- What might be the consequences of choosing the 'fail' bottle?
- How would you act in the same situation?
- In real life, do we ever face choices like the two-bottle choice?

- What dreams do you have?
- What helps you to succeed and to fulfil your dreams?
- What gets in the way of fulfilling your dreams?

- Create a different choice for the boy, together with a possible solution: retell the story with different bottles that have different properties and for which different rules must be followed.
- What changes does the boy have to get used to during the story?
- What are the boy's main skills and his personal qualities?

Adapt and apply:

Would You Rather,
John Burningham,
Red Fox, 1994

The Time Traveler's Wife,
Audrey Nifenegger,
MacAdam/Cage, 2003

Starting school	Use an age-appropriate story about decision-making such as *Would You Rather* by John Burningham. Ask children to dream up new decisions to make.
Moving year groups	Use the story to think about aspirations for the coming year.
Moving to secondary school	Focus on three things: the leaving-home aspect of the story, dreams of success and independent decision-making.
Unexpected moves	Depending on the nature and context of the move, use the story to help express feelings. Fairytale motifs map children's psychological development. Use other tales to acknowledge quietly and reflect on any challenges a child might be facing.
Starting college/university – leaving home	Use films/stories that deal with separation (such as *The Time Traveler's Wife*) to prompt discussion about transition to education away from home.

Custom certificates

Summary:
Bespoke certificates that celebrate and value the diverse skills and attitudes required at transition.

Activity:
Formal acknowledgement and validation of the qualities that will be needed for successful transition will help to give children proof that they will be OK. Imagine a child who is terribly anxious about going to secondary school being presented, in Year 6, with a certificate for 'Facing your fears and doing it anyway'. Imagine that same certificate displayed in that child's bedroom all through the summer and catching their eye as they leave for school on the first day of the new term in September.

Microsoft Word and other similar applications offer many certificate templates that can be customised quickly. The following page shows my example (94 seconds in the making). Below are suggestions for custom certificates for different types of transition.

Adapt and apply:

	Custom certificates for:
Starting school	Starting school, Making a friend, Learning the rules, Knowing what happens when, Making a good choice
Moving year groups	Successfully completing Year X, Using learning from Year X in Year X+1, Getting to know a new routine
Moving to secondary school	Expressing feelings clearly, Successful taster day / open day / summer camp / early-transition week, Confidence, Facing fears, Successfully completing primary school
Unexpected moves	Settling in, Making friends, Being confident and brave, Asking questions
Starting college/university – leaving home	Successfully completing secondary school / sixth form, Mistake of the week, Quirk of the month, Talent of the term, Packing for uni. (by this age, students will respond to tongue-in-cheek certificates which nevertheless communicate praiseworthy qualities)

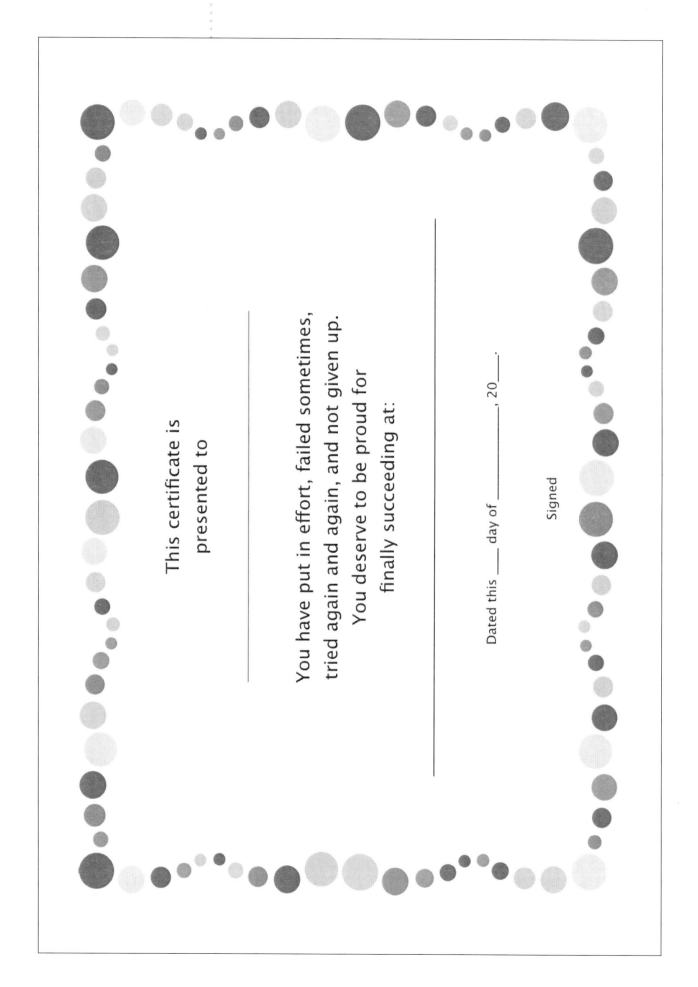

This certificate is
presented to

You have put in effort, failed sometimes,
tried again and again, and not given up.
You deserve to be proud for
finally succeeding at:

Dated this _____ day of _____, 20_____.

Signed

Learning detectives

Summary:
A pupil-driven analysis of learning and teaching styles which provides a benchmark against which they can compare future classroom experiences.

Activity:
Pupils' unique learning styles are fixed but include flexibility within certain boundaries. But the teaching styles they experience in different schools and classes will vary. Children need a language to talk about these differences.

Send pupils around the school with Learning Detective Record sheets (see page 42) to find out where and how they think learning is happening. Use their evidence to begin a discussion about teaching and learning styles and about what makes for good learning (and teaching).

Adapt and apply:

Starting school	Use signs and symbols to mark different types of activity and teacher interventions.
Moving year groups	Send pupils to investigate teaching and learning in the next year group.
Moving to secondary school	Ask ex-Year 7 pupils to collect evidence, then return to primary school and report to the Year 6 children.
Unexpected moves	Give pupils the option to observe the class first before joining in.
Starting college/university – leaving home	Invite student ambassadors to visit and describe learning and teaching styles at university.

Learning Detective Record

Herewith, evidence collected by _____
on this _____ day of _____, 20____
presented as proof that learning may be, or may have been,
happening at _____ school.

I saw teachers:

using computers and whiteboards		watching what's going on	
using their arms and hands to explain		thinking	
smiling / with different expressions		writing or drawing	
moving around the class		working and learning	
marking work		letting pupils take over the lesson.	

I saw pupils:

working on their own		listening to each other	
working in pairs		listening to a teacher	
working in groups		smiling	
writing or drawing		moving around	
using computers		concentrating.	

I heard teachers:

explaining to the whole class		using different voices	
explaining to a group		using interesting words	
explaining to one person		being enthusiastic	
asking *what* and *when* questions		laughing	
asking *how* and *why* and *what if*		answering questions.	

I heard pupils:

teaching each other		asking for help	
asking *what* and *when* questions		answering questions	
asking *how* and *why* and *what if*		thinking out loud	
using interesting words		checking what to do	
laughing		saying 'learning'.	

Further evidence that learning **has** happened: _____

Further evidence that learning **is** happening: _____

Patchworks

Summary:
A thinking skills activity in which pupils make creative connections between the diverse elements of a transition experience.

Activity:
Give pupils (individuals, pairs or groups) a copy of the Patchwork squares sheet (see page 44). Ask them to find connections between neighbouring squares. Then get them to cut out all the squares and rearrange them into a line so that each square has a creative connection to the next. Finally they attempt to link the first and last squares.

Adapt and apply:

Starting school	Use symbols or picture cards and ask pupils to link them by similar characteristics (colours, etc.) or to assemble them into stories.
Moving year groups	Customise the squares to the next year group – use the names of teachers and mention any likely differences from the current year.
Moving to secondary school	Use as is and then extend the idea by creating a real patchwork quilt celebrating each member of the year group.
Unexpected moves	Customise the squares so that they relate directly to the main features of the school, such as teachers, location, clubs – the things you want the new arrival to know.
Starting college/university – leaving home	Customise the squares for university – include 'lectures', 'independence', 'student union', etc.

Patchworks

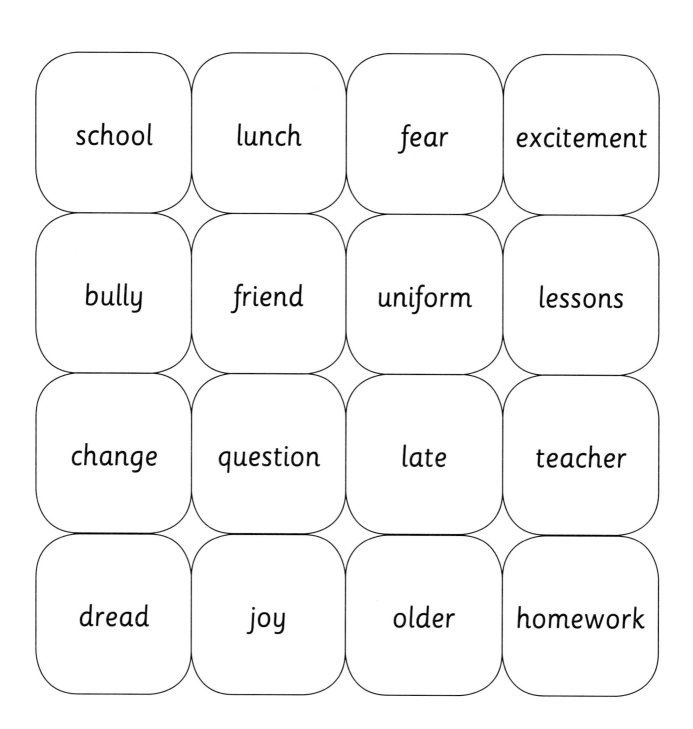

school	lunch	fear	excitement
bully	friend	uniform	lessons
change	question	late	teacher
dread	joy	older	homework

Video questions

Summary:
A thinking and questioning activity based on short (animated) films.
Appropriate films are chosen for age and type of transition.

Activity:
Show the film you've chosen and afterwards ask individuals to write down one question about what they've seen. Then ask pupils to pair up and decide which of their two questions would be harder to answer. Challenge them to think up two new questions: one that would be harder to answer than either of their original ones, and one that would be easier. Each pair now has four questions. Pairs then join into fours, swap questions and attempt to answer them. Use the discussions to draw out transition and other issues.

Adapt and apply:
There is a wealth of short films online. Below is one suggestion for each type of transition, with its title and focus. I can't guarantee you'll be able to find them exactly where I did, but Google, You Tube and the title should get you there. Always watch films first to check for suitability.

Starting school	*Kiwi!*, a 3-minute film about a bird who learns to fly (sort of).
Moving year groups	*Simon's Cat Snow Business*, a 2-minute film in which Simon's cat explores a new environment.
Moving to secondary school	*Big Buck Bunny*, a 10-minute film about bullying in the forest.
Unexpected moves	*The Lucky Dip*, a 3-minute film about how people and rabbits aren't always what they seem.
Starting college/university – leaving home	*Perfeito*, a 3-minute film about the perils of seeking perfection.

Activities for during transition

Journey sticks

Summary:
A creative and artistic task in which pupils make a representation of a story or journey, and then use it to retell the story.

Activity:
A journey stick is used to retell the story of a journey. Along the way, bits and pieces tied to the stick represent events, feelings and milestones. When the journey is over the bits and pieces tied to the stick prompt the retelling of what has happened.

Use real sticks together with objects, photos and craft materials; or use instead a drawing of a stick, a piece of rope or a cardboard tube.

Adapt and apply:

Starting school	Liaise with nursery or home and have children bring journey sticks into school that have features attached to represent significant aspects of home/ nursery. Children talk about their sticks and add to them.
Moving year groups	Liaise with colleagues and have children bring journey sticks to a new school year that have features attached to represent aspects of the previous year. Children talk about their sticks and add to them.
Moving to secondary school	Liaise across schools and have Year 6 children bring journey sticks to a taster day that have features attached to represent aspects of primary school. Or use journey sticks to sum up primary-school life.
Unexpected moves	Liaise with parents/agencies and have children use journey sticks to represent their story.
Starting college/university – leaving home	Students create journey sticks to summarise their learning journeys from the time they began school until now.

Wikispaces

Summary:
Online collaborative spaces for sharing information essential to transition. For use before, during and after a move.

Activity:
Already mentioned under Wikispace video projects (see page 29), this free online resource may be adapted to many different transition uses: www.wikispaces.com

Adapt and apply:

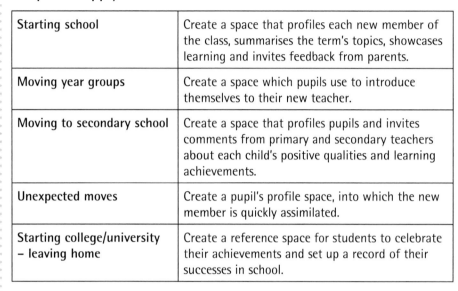

Starting school	Create a space that profiles each new member of the class, summarises the term's topics, showcases learning and invites feedback from parents.
Moving year groups	Create a space which pupils use to introduce themselves to their new teacher.
Moving to secondary school	Create a space that profiles pupils and invites comments from primary and secondary teachers about each child's positive qualities and learning achievements.
Unexpected moves	Create a pupil's profile space, into which the new member is quickly assimilated.
Starting college/university – leaving home	Create a reference space for students to celebrate their achievements and set up a record of their successes in school.

Dreamboard

Summary:

A visual collage that showcases personal dreams and aspirations in five categories.

Activity:

Pupils use images from magazines and the internet, together with personal photos and drawings, to crystallise their dreams and aspirations into a single striking collage. Using A3 as a minimum size, they should assemble images to the following template:

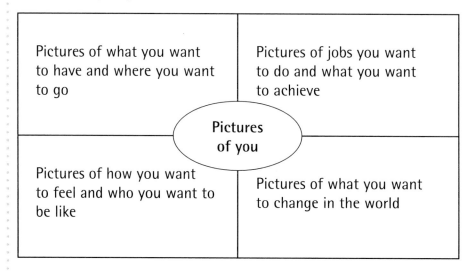

The board may be gradually filled over time and during transition. As dreams are fulfilled and aspirations met, new images may be pasted over the old.

Adapt and apply:

Starting school	Customise dreamboard categories as appropriate. Include 'What I want to be', 'What I want to have', 'What I want to be like.'
Moving year groups	Pupils use their dreamboards to express who they are to their new teacher.
Moving to secondary school	Use dreamboards to straddle the summer transition, and include a category related to secondary school.
Unexpected moves	Create a dreamboard with a new arrival to explore their culture, background and experience of life and learning.
Starting college/university – leaving home	Photograph dreamboards, minimise and laminate to credit-card size. Students carry their dreams around with them and on to university.

VoiceThread

Summary:
A collaborative online space that encourages video, audio and text comments.

Activity:
Set up a VoiceThread (voicethread.com) with a clear purpose and rules for contribution. A VoiceThread is a linear, evolving conversation that can map a transition journey as well as a voyage through the curriculum. Teachers initiate a dialogue with prompt questions and images to which invited pupils may respond. Their combined responses prompt the next image, about which further comments are made, and so the thread begins. The whole journey may be revisited at any time by any of the contributors.

Adapt and apply:

Starting school	Create a VoiceThread to describe the first few weeks of school and encourage parents to contribute, with their child, from home.
Moving year groups	Create a VoiceThread to describe the last few weeks of one school year and first few weeks of the next.
Moving to secondary school	Create a VoiceThread to describe the last few weeks of primary school, the summer holidays and the first few weeks at secondary school.
Unexpected moves	Create a VoiceThread to describe the first few weeks in a new school with contributions from a child's parents/carers.
Starting college/university – leaving home	Create a VoiceThread to describe the last few weeks of school, summer holiday activities and starting university.

101Q thinking

Summary:

A method of capturing existing questions and generating many new ones. Transition prompts many questions which, when answered, may go a long way to setting pupils' minds at rest. 101Q thinking is a technique for having fun with questions. The challenge (in this case) is to generate 101 questions about the particular transition. After transition, the questions may be revisited and possibly answered.

Activity:

The system is pretty simple: pupils use a variety of categories, generating a handful of questions for each category. Ten questions in each of ten different categories is a hundred questions – only one to go.

Give groups ten minutes to write down 101 different questions about their upcoming transition. Typical prompt categories for moving to secondary school are: Subjects (What subject will I study?); Teachers (How many teachers will I have?); Clubs (Is there a basketball club?); Lessons (How long are lessons?); Timetable (Is there any free time?).

Adapt and apply:

Starting school	Model the asking and answering of questions and encourage pupils to ask many questions about their new school.
Moving year groups	Focus questions on the next year group.
Moving to secondary school	Ask questions about secondary school and attempt to answer them after transition.
Unexpected moves	Create space and time for new arrivals to find out as much as they want to about their new environment.
Starting college/university – leaving home	101 questions about university.

Activities for after transition

The art of memory

Summary:

The art of memory is a collection of ancient recall techniques still used in the present day. One of the most effective is 'architectural mnemonic', a process of associating a sequence of memories with the features of a building or an outdoor space. By repeatedly walking through the building following the same route, sequential memory is laid down. Recalling the route later, and in a different place, will activate the memories associated with various parts of the building.

Activity:

The size and scale of a setting may be a major concern for pupils who are new to it. 'Where am I supposed to be and how do I get there?' are frequent worries. A tour will typically take in most parts of the environment only once. For architectural mnemonics the suggestion is that the tour route should be repeated with pauses at significant places.

Plan your tour for new pupils, and identify ten key stops and something memorable at each one. At each place point out the memorable feature and have pupils repeat it to each other. Once the tour has finished, invite pupils to repeat it either on their own or with other pupils present on call. If time allows, repeat. Finally have pupils describe the route and its milestones to each other in glorious detail.

Adapt and apply:

Starting school	Tours around the class or part of the school.
Moving year groups	Tours around the new class – resources/routines.
Moving to secondary school	Tours around the new school.
Unexpected moves	Tours guided by greeter pupils.
Starting college/university – leaving home	Tours organised by student ambassadors.

Graffiti wall

Summary:

A large-group collaborative task for sharing ideas which leads into individual reflection and then small-group discussion.

Activity:

Stick lengths of lining paper around your room/hall. Give each pupil a pen and ask them to write on the paper any questions, concerns or ideas they have about their new environment. Do this in silence or with quiet music playing. After a suitable time ask pupils to stop and return to their seats.

After sharing several contributions made on the graffiti wall, they return to the wall and collect the three questions/concerns/ideas that are most personally relevant to them and use these in a group discussion. If several pupils want to choose the same or similar combinations, either encourage them to write their own copies or give them time to collect different ideas.

Adapt and apply:

Starting school	Draw favourite things on the graffiti wall.
Moving year groups	Write expectations for the new year on the graffiti wall.
Moving to secondary school	Write concerns on the graffiti wall.
Unexpected moves	–
Starting college/university – leaving home	Write significant moments on the graffiti wall.

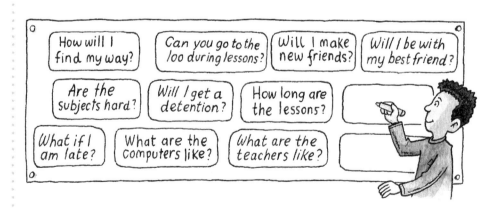

Open graph

Summary:
A high-order thinking skills activity in which information is missed off a graph or chart to prompt thinking about what the graph might show.

Activity:
Show one or more of the graphs on page 54. Tell pupils that the graphs give important information about the school, and they must work out what it is. The titles and axes detail is missing. Pupils discuss possible interpretations in groups by speculating about what the titles and axes might be.

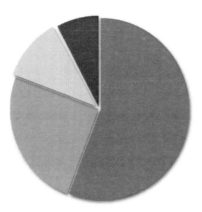

Adapt and apply:

Starting school	Introduce pictograms showing simple school facts.
Moving year groups	The open graph(s) describe features of the new year group.
Moving to secondary school	The open graph(s) describe features of the new school.
Unexpected moves	The open graph(s) describe features of the new school.
Starting college/university – leaving home	The open graph(s) describe features of university.

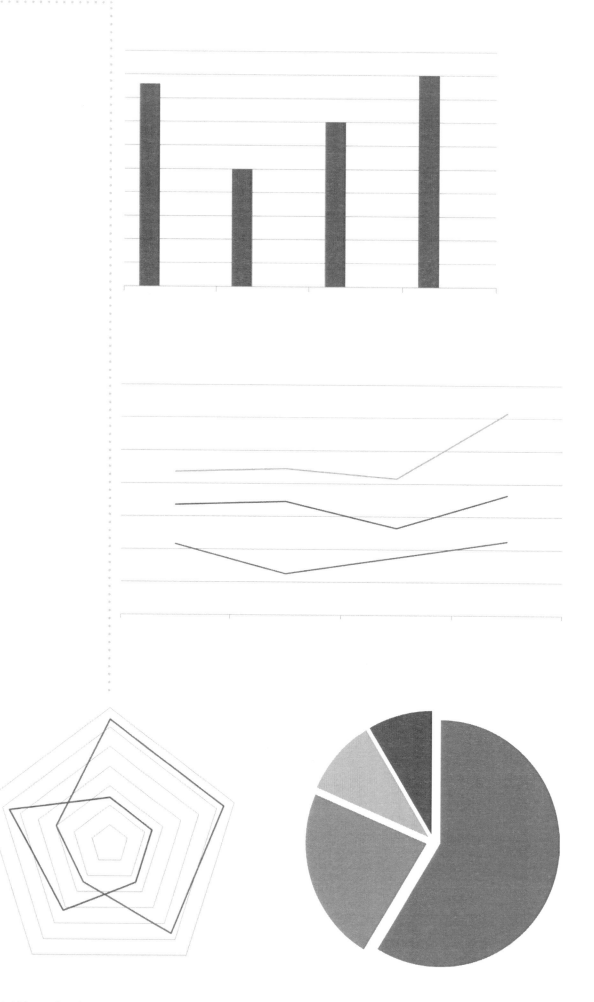

Home team

Summary:
A task roles and bonding activity to support group work.

Activity:
Lots of the activities in this section and those commonly found in transition programmes rely on effective group and team work. Have pupils negotiate the roles shown on page 56 and then complete the simple task below. If they cannot decide among themselves who is to take each role, assign these yourself.

Home team task:

- ◯ Clarify task role responsibilities.

- ◯ Take turns to tell each other your name, favourite thing (TV show / game / food – anything), age and number of pets.

- ◯ Create a two-part group name that includes only letters from your own first names (repeats allowed). The name must itself comprise a first and last name.

- ◯ Add up your ages.

- ◯ Add up the number of pets you have.

- ◯ Prepare a presentation as if your group is a giant person:

    - ○ Include the group name, total ages, total pets and combined favourite things and speak in unison.

    - ○ For example: (group of six Year 7s all speaking together)
      'Hello, I am Cordy Drool. I'm 68 years old, I have 12 pets and I like Jesse J, Pizza, Minecraft, more Pizza, Coke and football.''

Adapt and apply:

Starting school	Pairs alternate the roles of talker and listener and tell each other about themselves.
Moving year groups	Adapt/reduce roles and task to be age appropriate.
Moving to secondary school	As above during induction.
Unexpected moves	Use to include and introduce mid-year joiners.
Starting college/university – leaving home	As above during freshers' week, but with additional success criteria involving the inclusion of singing, acting and poor jokes.

Task Roles

Timekeeper

Timekeeper thinks about time and manages it for the group

★ Know when the activity starts and finishes
★ Help the facilitator to plan the activity and use the time well
★ Tell the group how long is left

Facilitator

Facilitator thinks about the whole group and manages the task and the learning

★ Make sure everyone has a job to do and feels included
★ Plan the activity with the timekeeper's help
★ Tell the group what's happening and why

Recorder

Recorder thinks about making notes and writing or drawing for the group

★ Make notes about group discussions
★ Be responsible for any written or visual work that needs to be done
★ Work with the reporter – who will have to read from your notes

Reporter

Reporter thinks about speaking and talks on behalf of the group

★ Work with the recorder to make sure you can use their notes/diagrams
★ Make sure you speak for the group and not just yourself
★ Ask questions on behalf of the group

Resourcer

Resourcer thinks about materials and equipment and manages these for group

★ Collect the tools, equipment and materials needed by the group
★ Make sure that the working area is kept clean, safe and tidy
★ Only take what your group needs and no more

Checker

Checker thinks about the quality of what's being made and how

★ Make sure you know what the group is supposed to be making/doing
★ Tell the group what they've done well and what needs to be improved
★ Make sure each person is sticking to their group role

Speed lines

Summary:

A large-group speaking and listening activity that introduces pupils to each other, breaks the ice and builds confidence.

Activity:

- ◗ Arrange pupils facing each other in two lines of equal length. Everyone is facing their partner.

- ◗ Give everyone 30 seconds to tell their partner their name and any two things about themselves, and then to hear the same from their partner.

- ◗ After 30 seconds the person at the end of one line is directed to walk down between both lines and to join the other end of their line.

- ◗ On this signal, everyone in that line moves one place up and thus gains a new partner.

- ◗ These new pairings share the same information and after 30 more seconds the shuffle-up move is repeated.

- ◗ This happens three or four more times, after which everyone has talked about themselves and heard about four or five other people.

Adapt and apply:

Starting school	Work in pairs or fours and develop basic turn taking.
Moving year groups	Use to share expectations for the new year group.
Moving to secondary school	Use during induction week to get pupils talking and sharing.
Unexpected moves	Use to introduce a new member of the class carefully.
Starting college/university – leaving home	Use to make friends during freshers' week.

Section 5
Next steps

Maintaining the transition advantage

When educational transitions are managed effectively, pupils can maximise the time and effort they put into the business of learning, rather than using that same energy in dealing with orientation, friendship and learning-style issues. And as each set of five bridges is crossed successfully, students leaving school for college, university or work can do so with more confidence and a greater ability to handle further change that will inevitably come their way.

It's therefore important that each new transition makes reference to previous ones; for example: 'Remember when you started school, well this is similar, but you'll be going to a bigger school now ... Remember how you felt, and how it was OK in the end? Well, it'll be the same this time!'

In an ideal world, a transition programme develops progressively right the way through a pupil's school career, each move building on the previous one – a challenge to organise, yet in principle the basics could readily be set up. For example, a Personal Learning Profile (see pages 21–26) could track a pupil from 3 to 18 in addition to any grades they pick up along the way. The Personal Learning Profile provides an evolving continuity that describes the pupil as a learner rather than as a series of numbers and letters.

Moving to college or university

You've got to do your own growing, no matter how tall your grandfather was.

Irish proverb

I've attempted to give you ideas and activities which, by and large, can be used in any transition. Inevitably the move from primary to secondary gets most of the attention, yet the move from secondary is equally important. This is a final staging post before university/college or work and it requires a change in style and attitude for which learners need adequate preparation.

Here are the reflections of three students from The Westgate School in Winchester (see impact study, page 13) who are about to leave Year 11 and begin A Level courses at Peter Symonds, a local sixth-form college. None of the three girls had a standard start to secondary school, either arriving after Year 7, or coming from well out of the catchment area and knowing none or only a handful of fellow pupils. Use the prompt questions with your own learners to help them prepare for a move and connect with previous transitions.

It's fascinating to read that the students' fears are similar in nature yet different in content to the fears engendered by other transitions.

What are your thoughts/feelings about leaving Westgate?

It's exciting to have the chance for a fresh start and leave any mistakes (like dying your hair bright ginger) behind. But at the same time it's completely nerve racking to think of all the new and wonderful mistakes we'll get to make in front of a bunch of strangers over the next two years. On top of that is the worry that you'll lose touch with people who've played such a massive part over the past quarter of our lives.

I think I'm ready to leave Westgate. It feels like the right time for a change now, although it is quite scary. Being at Westgate for five years is the longest I've ever been at one school and I'm really used to being there, so being at college is going to be different. The best thing is knowing that once I've left school I'll only be studying the subjects I'm really interested in and enjoy.

I think I will miss Westgate, but I am looking forward to being able to focus on the studies I enjoy and want to carry on with and having the opportunity to study photography. I am glad that college releases some of the restrictions on what you wear and what you look like that Westgate enforces.

What are your thoughts/feelings/worries/expectations about going to sixth-form college?

It's so exciting to get to drop maths! It's great that I get to spend so many hours a week on the things I actually love (nerd moment). At the same time I'm definitely terrified/excited about all of the new scary teenagers, but again it's a great chance, hopefully, to meet people who'll be interested in the same subjects.

It's nice to know that there will be lots of people around college that I will know from school, so I'm not worried about not knowing people even though there may be nobody I know in any of my classes. It will be a good opportunity to make new friends with people who are interested in similar things to me. I'm most worried that I have not made the right subject choices. I'm scared I will get halfway through the first year and hate all my classes and not be able to do anything about it. These decisions would have been easier if I knew what job I wanted as then I would at least know that what I was doing was necessary for my future career. It has been hard to make subject choices without knowing my end goal and you always feel as if teachers expect you to know.

I am worried about the huge number of students that Peter Symonds College has and the workload for my coursework subjects, but I hope to gain confidence and most importantly knowledge so I can become a forensic photographer.

How well do you feel the transition between Y11 and Y12 has been organised and managed by school or college?

It's been run really smoothly by Westgate because it's a feeder school to Symonds and it's just round the corner. It was so easy because the interviewers came to Westgate and we got all the forms by parentmail and so on, and we constantly had our teachers from Westgate telling us exactly what to do and how.

The only down side to the transition is that it was so easy that I don't think we'll be prepared for applying to university!

I think it is handled really smoothly, especially with Symonds as it is so close to school. But all the colleges have been really good, doing talks in school, open evenings and lots of information has been available at interviews. The only thing I don't like about the transition is that, even though I've finished my exams, my place at Symonds is not guaranteed till two weeks before the start of term. This leaves lots of time to worry about not having the grades to get in.

I feel Westgate gives you some support if you choose Peter Symonds or other catchment colleges. Also I feel more comfortable about going to Peter Symonds as they gave lots more information and were positive and honest during my interview. But I don't feel challenged by college as it is so close to my secondary school.

What do you remember about your transition from primary to secondary?

Not a lot to be honest — I guess I had a pretty unique experience. First I missed the second half of Year 6 because of heart surgery and then post-surgery complications, then straight after that we moved from Australia to Winchester, which was doubly confusing because the school year starts in September (rather than at the beginning of each calendar year). So I was effectively thrown into Year 7 in the middle of June with no experience of secondary school whatsoever. It was horrific — not recommended. The grading system was completely different and I don't think I understand the whole 5a/4b thing now! I don't think anyone realised I had just come from primary school, so it took me a while to get my head around 'tutor time' and different classrooms. I think everyone will agree that secondary school feels a lot bigger than primary, only when you're in Year 7 the Year 11s seem a lot scarier than Year 6s. (The irony is that as a nerdy Year 11, the 'cool' Year 7s terrified me!)

The main thing I remember is that my junior school wasn't very involved with the move. This may have been as I was not going to a feeder school, but they didn't seem to be much help to the majority of my class that were going to feeder schools. Like me, the only information they got came from the secondary school. In my opinion that information came too late as most of it came only a month before finishing junior school and that seemed a very long time after getting a place (it left lots of time to worry about things). However, I did go on a summer camp at Westgate and that was great because I got to make friends. I was the only person from my school going to Westgate.

Due to my goldfish memory, very little. But I was excited as I had been doing Year 7 work in Year 6 which was helpful and boosted my confidence about going to a new school. I was upset that I wasn't in a tutor group with my best friend but having a twin brother in the same tutor group helped me break off to make new friends.

Do you notice any similarities between Year 6–7 transition and Year 11–12 transition?

Honestly, I can't really say my teachers prepared me for moving to an English secondary school ... Though from what I remember it was similar in the way that the open days were run and we had orientation days to get to know the school and a few subjects of your choice, and my primary and secondary were pretty local to each other, so there was a lot of collaboration to make it easier.

No. The only thing that is the same is the transition bit. But I am moving with friends, which makes a difference.

Some in the sense that we are changing schools, but the pressure to get good results to be able to get into a good college is huge.

Few things are more satisfying than seeing your own children have teenagers of their own.

Doug Larson

Final comment

Planned and unplanned change is inevitable in our lives and in the lives of our learners. We give them a great and lasting gift when we teach them about change and when we give them the right support through it.

Please use the principles and practices in this book to embed an understanding of educational transitions into your thinking and into your day-to-day practice, and by all means take the ideas out of school and use them to manage your own personal and professional growth. Do let me know how you get on! Comments, questions and ideas to mike@thinkingclassroom.co.uk.

References

Paul Blagburn and Sophie Cloutterbuck (eds), *A Multi-disciplinary Approach to supporting Student Transition into Higher Education: a pilot study*, London Metropolitan University, *Investigations in University Teaching and Learning*, vol. 7, spring 2011; available online.

Maurice Galton, John Gray and Jean Ruddock, *The Impact of School Transition and Transfers on Pupil Progress and Attainment*, Research Report 131, Homerton College, Cambridge; available online.

Selected further resources

Here are sources of further ideas and activities that may be applied to transition programmes.

www.thinkingclassroom.co.uk:
Mike Fleetham's popular website offering free and premium classroom resources and monthly lesson plans.

A companion book to this one:
Ainsley Dawrent, *Successful School Transition* LDA (2008).

Support for parents:
Mollie Potter, *Parent's Survival Guide to Starting Secondary School: Ease the Transition for You and Your Child!*, A. & C. Black Publishers Ltd (2011).

For schools and for parents of children with Specific Learning Difficulties preparing to move to secondary school:
The Dyscovery Centre, *Top Tips for Transition: Ensuring a successful move to secondary school for children with Specific Learning Difficulties.*
This booklet can be purchased for £1 + postage from The Dyscovery Centre, University of Wales, Newport, NP20 5DA;
email: dyscoverycentre@newport.ac.uk

Understanding teenagers:
Stephen R. Covey, *The 7 Habits of Highly Effective Teens: The Ultimate Teenage Success Guide*, Simon & Schuster Ltd (2004).

Getting learners engaged with school:
Alan McLean, *Motivating Every Learner*, Sage (2009).

How to
support children
moving school

Mike Fleetham

Acknowledgements

For offering their time, experience and opinions about transition:

Students: Molly Bevan, Ben Cawston, Katherine Crawford, Tom Crozier, Christian Dawson, Ella Fleetham, Ellan Gillett, Joe Conroy Helstrip, Zac Henry, Jack Jones, James Maddocks, Lola Matthews, Iain Reeves, Theo Servimi, David Shaw, Chloe Sidhu, Harriet Spelman, Amelia Spence, Mollie Stannard, Alice Taylor, Theo Trebacz, Theo Webb.

Teachers: Heather Baldwin (headteacher, White House Primary School, Hailsham), Christopher Egerton Chesney (headmaster, Foxborough Primary School), Claire Fyvie-Rae (The Westgate School, Winchester), Gareth Jones (Hailsham Community College), Helen Riddall (White House Primary).

LDA has a range of learning development aids to help children with special needs and general learning difficulties. For our full range and helpful information visit www.ldalearning.com.

Permission to photocopy

This book contains materials which may be reproduced by photocopier or other means for use by the purchaser. The permission is granted on the understanding that these copies will be used within the educational establishment of the purchaser. The book and all its contents remain copyright. Copies may be made without reference to the publisher or the licensing scheme for the making of photocopies operated by the Publishers' Licensing Agency.

The right of Mike Fleetham to be identified as the author of this work has been asserted by him in accordance with sections 77 and 78 of the Copyright, Designs and Patents Act 1988.

How to support children moving school
ISBN: 978-1-85503-552-2

© Mike Fleetham
Cover illustration by Robin Edmonds
Inside illustrations by Garry Davies
All rights reserved
First published 2013. Reprinted 2013

Printed in the UK for LDA
LDA, Findel Education, Hyde Buildings, Ashton Road, Hyde, Cheshire, SK14 4SH